To a fragile baby, whom Mother Teresa would have regarded
with tenderness, as a masterpiece of God.
C. G.

To all those who fight injustice.
C. C.

The editor would like to thank the Mother Teresa of Calcutta Center (Mexico)
and the Missionaries of Charity Brothers (District 15 of Paris) for their help.

Under the direction of Romain Lizé, Vice President, Magnificat
Editor, Magnificat: Isabelle Galmiche
Editor, Ignatius: Vivian Dudro
Assistant to the Editor: Pascale van de Walle
Layout Designer: Elena Germain
Production: Thierry Dubus, Sabine Marioni

Original French edition: Mère Teresa, le sourire de Calcutta
© 2010 by Mame, Paris.

Printed in June 2016 by Tien Wah Press, Malaysia
Job number MGN 16014
Printed in compliance with the Consumer Protection Safety Act, 2008.

The Life of a Saint

Mother Teresa
The Smile of Calcutta

Text: Charlotte Grossetête - Illustrations: Catherine Chion
Translated by Janet Chevrier

MAGNIFICAT · Ignatius

"Come, be my light!"

$\mathcal{L}$and! The boat was about to arrive in Dublin, Ireland. With a lump in her throat, a young Albanian woman gazed at the approaching harbor. At eighteen, Gonxha had bid farewell to her family. She had crossed the whole of Europe to join the Sisters of Loreto!

Another lady passenger also waiting to land said to her, "You've come a long way."

"I hope to go even farther," Gonxha replied. "My dream is to become a missionary."

But would the mother superior think her strong enough to be sent to a faraway land? Gonxha was small, thin, and in delicate health. But she had so much trust in God!

A few months later, another boat was landing in Calcutta, a big city in India. On board, Gonxha was singing. She was so happy. It was here that she was to become a nun for ever.

And so, Gonxha, who had received the name Sister Mary Teresa, discovered India. In Calcutta, many people lived in poverty, crowded into slums of rickety, dirty huts. What a shock for Sister Teresa to see swarms of begging, barefoot children, dying old men being ignored by everyone, bustling people trying their best to earn their daily bread!

But it was not to the poorest people in the streets that the young woman was sent: Sister Teresa became a teacher in a Calcutta high school for girls run by the Sisters of Loreto.

"I'm the happiest of the sisters," she sometimes wrote to her mother. She loved her new life; she was content to work wherever God sent her. After six years she was given the title of Mother. Seven years later she became the school principal. Little did she suspect that one day God would give her a different mission.

In 1946, Mother Teresa boarded a train. Just as every year, she was going to pray and rest for a few days in Darjeeling, at the foot of the Himalaya Mountains.

Smoke billowed from the steam engine. Seated on a wooden bench, crowded between other lady travelers, Mother Teresa prayed to Jesus, as she was wont to do.

And suddenly, Jesus answered her! She heard his voice in her heart:

"Come to me in the poorest of the poor"

Stunned, Mother Teresa spent whole days praying to understand this call. Jesus explained to her:

"I want Indian nuns, Missionaries of Charity, to be my fire of love among the very poor, the sick, the dying, and the little children of the streets."

Everything became clear. Mother Teresa must leave her convent and live among the poor. That frightened her: she did not feel strong enough for this mission. Why had God chosen her? But a promise from Jesus reassured her: "I will always be with you."

However, a nun cannot leave her convent just like that, without permission. So Mother Teresa told the whole story to Father Van Exem, who knew her well. He asked her to write to the bishop of Calcutta.

What a surprise for the bishop to receive her request! Never had a foreign nun wished to live in the slums, dressed in a sari like an Indian woman.

"Who is this woman? How can I be sure this plan is from God?" wondered Archbishop Ferdinand Périer.

He thought and prayed a very long time. A bishop must be careful before granting anyone permission to found a new religious community!

Waiting for the archbishop's decision was hard for Mother Teresa. She was eager to carry out her mission, to do what Jesus was asking of her. But she knew that God's will is found through obedience to proper authority. So Mother Teresa prayed and hoped.

At last, Mother Teresa received permission to leave her convent. She arrived in the slums of Calcutta, dressed in a white sari with a blue border, all alone, without anything to offer the thousands who live and sleep in the streets. She breathed in the terrible smell of the sewers, she was jostled by rickshaws. Her head was spinning.

"Where to begin?"

She had learned a few nursing skills, but one woman alone would never be enough to care for so many sick and dying people!

But she was there at God's invitation, and she believed nothing is impossible for God. So, with great courage, she moved in with a family who lent her two small rooms on the third floor of their house. And she set to work.

The months went by. Mother Teresa worked hard.

Missionary of Charity

"Hello, Mother. Do you recognize me? I'm Subashini Das, one of your old students."

"Of course! How are you, Subashini? How kind of you to visit me."

"I haven't come to visit. I'd like to share in your life."

Mother Teresa looked at the young woman's manicured hands. Subashini was from a wealthy family: she knew nothing of life in these filthy streets.

"You know, Subashini, life is horrible here—"

"Accept me, I beg of you. I will not shrink from any work, even if it's difficult."

And so Mother Teresa welcomed her first sister with joy. They were very soon joined by other young women. The community of the Missionaries of Charity was born!

Soon, everyone in Calcutta recognized these women in white saris who cared for the poor of the slums day in and day out. In order to live like the people they served, they wished to own as little as possible and to live very simply.

Each morning when it was still dark, the sisters went to the chapel. Kneeling among her sisters, Mother Teresa prayed in silence. She loved to pray to the Virgin Mary:

"Mother, it is you who are the source of my joy, because you gave the world Jesus. I in turn wish to be your joy, by serving the poor and giving them Jesus."

After morning prayers, the sisters attended Mass together. Then, two by two, they would go out into the slum. Mother Teresa encouraged them in her warm voice:

"In the Host, we have received Jesus. He is the Bread of Life. Now, go out in search of the 'hungry Jesus' hidden inside each one of the poor whom we will serve today!"

The sisters tenderly nursed the sickest of people, especially those who had no one to care for them. They took care of lepers, who were often despised in India because their disease was considered a punishment from God.

They also tended to those suffering from loneliness, neglect, and despair.

One day, Mother Teresa was crossing Calcutta. The car horns beeping, the children crying, the beggars calling out—the thousand noises of the slum were familiar to her now! Suddenly, she noticed an old woman on the point of death with no one paying her any attention.

Gently, Mother Teresa bent down, got the woman to her feet, and took her to the hospital.

"We can't do anything for her," said the doctor. "There's no hope for her."

"But we can't just let her die in the street!" cried Mother Teresa.

"You can see that the hospital's overflowing with sick people already. It is out of the question to give up beds to the dying!"

Mother Teresa found herself outside again with the old woman. Her heart sank.

"Too many of the poor die with no one to take care of them," she thought to herself. "Their lives have been so difficult; they at least should be given the chance to die in peace!"

Mother Teresa had an idea. So she went to see the city authorities.

"Please give me a place where I can receive the dying. My sisters and I will care for them to the end."

The people at the town hall considered her request:

"We can lend you a pilgrim shelter, next to the temple of the goddess Kali."

Soon afterward, rows of cots were set up in the refuge, from then on known as Nirmal Hriday, which means "pure heart." The sunlight shone through the large windows of the two rooms: peace reigned at Nirmal Hriday, despite the noise of the city.

Each morning, the sisters toured the slums picking up the most seriously ill in ambulances.

They would take them to Nirmal Hriday, where they washed them, made them comfortable, and held their hand until they departed to be with God. No, the sisters could not cure them. But they could at least care for them and surround them with love.

But the Hindu priests who served the goddess Kali were furious to have these Christian nuns as neighbors, and they went to complain at the town hall.

"These foreigners have no business being here."

"They're not foreigners," they were told. "Mother Teresa has been granted Indian citizenship, and her sisters are Indians too."

"That makes no difference!" the priests said. "All they want is to draw Indians into their religion."

They complained so much, the chief of police agreed to go to Nirmal Hriday to kick the sisters out. The priests waited for him outside, eager for him to carry out his mission!

A few moments later, the door opened. The Hindu priests, expecting to see all the sisters come out, were there ready to hurl insults at them. But the police chief emerged alone, moved by what he had seen in the hospice for the dying.

He said:

"The day your mothers and your sisters accept doing what these women do, then we'll see. In the meantime, the nuns are staying here."

Mother Teresa also gathered in little children. In India, many babies are abandoned at birth: babies that seem very frail, whose parents think themselves too poor to bring them up.

When the police would find one of these little ones in the street, they considered between themselves:

"What are we going to do with this one?"

"Let's take him to Mother Teresa."

"We have no right! You need permission from the government to adopt a child."

"Yes, but with the sisters, this baby will be loved, won't live in the street, will be given a future. That's what's most important, isn't it?"

So the policemen would go quietly to knock on the door of the Missionaries of Charity with their precious bundle in their arms.

When they saw that the work of Mother Teresa was proper and effective, the government no longer bothered the sisters. The sisters took good care of everyone, whether very young or very old.

An Unshakable Joy

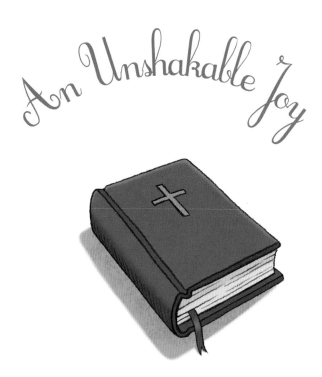

The Missionaries of Charity became more and more numerous. Mother Teresa watched over each one of them.

"Smile at someone, visit him, light a fire for someone who is cold, read something to someone. These are little things, very little, but they will make your love of God grow stronger," she told them.

The sisters listened in silence.

"You can pray by working. It's enough to turn toward Jesus and say, 'I love you, my God, I have trust in you, I believe in you, I need you.' Little things as simple as that. These are wonderful prayers."

Jesus! He was Mother Teresa's great love. When she spoke, it was always for him, with him in mind.

And yet, Mother Teresa experienced a great sorrow. Ever since she had moved to the slums, she no longer felt the presence of Jesus as she had before. She felt as though abandoned, rejected by him.

In her heart, she felt darkness and emptiness. She experienced the suffering of the poor who did not feel loved.

She shared in the loneliness Christ suffered on the Cross.

The priests she confided in reassured her. They knew that certain great saints had lived through this Dark Night and had accepted it as a trial sent by God to test their faithfulness.

Apart from these priests, no one else knew about her suffering. She did not want to sadden her sisters. Mother Teresa kept on smiling and courageously loving others: she remained confident in God. And so things would go on until her dying day!

Despite the Dark Night of her soul, Mother Teresa still believed in the power of prayer. To support the work of her sisters, she relied on sick or handicapped people who, unable to help the sisters in their daily work, accompanied them through prayer: they became known as the suffering cooperators.

The first of them was called Jacqueline. She was a Belgian nurse and a friend of Mother Teresa who would have liked to become a Missionary of Charity. But she was afflicted with a serious bone disease. So Mother Teresa wrote her a letter in which she explained that Jacqueline could still work with her. How? By offering her suffering for the poor and the unfortunate.

And so Jacqueline became inseparable from Mother Teresa, her twin sister in the eyes of God!

$\mathcal{A}$ided by the prayer of the suffering cooperators, the number of Missionaries of Charity grew and grew. Their communities spread throughout the world. They treat the ill everywhere, care for the dying, take in orphans, and aid the victims of war. The secret of their effectiveness is still prayer.

$\mathcal{M}$other Teresa became very famous. She traveled everywhere. Heads of state loved receiving her, journalists loved talking to her. This fame gave her no pleasure. She would have preferred to live secretly among the poor! But it was exactly for them that she accepted all these honors.

In December 1979, Mother Teresa found herself in Oslo, Norway, to receive the Nobel Peace Prize—the greatest award in the world to honor generous people! The streets were covered in snow. Wrapped in warm coats, a crowd of people applauded this tiny little nun in a sari. She had put on only a sweater to keep out the cold, and yet her immense smile warmed every heart!

Saint Pope John Paul II very soon became her close friend. He went to visit the hospice of Nirmal Hriday and was very impressed:

"Here, the dying can experience the love of God!" he said with admiration.

The years went by. Mother Teresa was now very old. Her health was worn out. She fell ill and suffered greatly. Her sisters worried, but Mother Teresa reassured them: she was eager to return to the house of God.

One day when she was in the hospital, the doctor said to a priest:

"Bring her that box she likes to have in her room."

"What box are you talking about?" asked the priest with surprise.

"A box she looks at all the time that brings her peace. I don't know what's in it."

That box was a tabernacle containing Jesus in the consecrated Host.

On September 5, 1997, Mother Teresa passed away at the age of eighty-seven. The government of India honored her with a state funeral, which was attended by 15,000 people. A million others lined the streets that day.

Mother Teresa's body was buried in the Mother House of the Missionaries of Charity in Calcutta. Her tomb quickly became a place of prayer for people of all faiths, rich and poor alike. Pope John Paul II called for her to be named a saint earlier than usual. "Let us welcome her message and follow her example," he said.

Feast Day

Mother Teresa is commemorated on September 5, the anniversary of her death. She was beatified in October 2003 by Pope Saint John Paul II, and canonized by Pope Francis in September 2016.

The Missionaries of Charity

The congregation of the Missionaries of Charity Sisters was officially established on October 7, 1950, in Calcutta.

Mother Teresa later founded:
- The Missionaries of Charity Brothers in 1963;
- The contemplative branch of the sisters in 1976 (they pray for the sisters working with the poor);
- The contemplative brothers in 1979;
- The Missionaries of Charity Fathers (priests) in 1984.

There are also **volunteers**: laypersons who assist the Missionaries of Charity.

The **cooperators** live in the spirit of Mother Teresa, pray for the Missionaries of Charity, and serve the poor.

Finally, the **suffering cooperators** offer up their illnesses and trials to God in prayer in support of the work of the Missionaries of Charity. Each has a counterpart within the community for whose work they commit themselves to pray.

Mother Teresa founded **houses** on every continent. The Missionaries of Charity Sisters number around 5,000 from about 100 different nationalities, spread throughout 765 houses, in 136 countries around the world. There are about 500 brothers.

The vocation of the Missionaries of Charity

The Missionaries of Charity give their lives to slake mankind's thirst for the love of Jesus. They are a symbol of divine compassion toward each person, seeking dignity for all. They make themselves "victims of love" to carry God among the poorest of the poor.

The sari

The Lord said to Mother Teresa, "You will dress in simple Indian garments or, rather, dress like my mother—in simplicity and poverty. . . . Your sari will become holy because it will be my symbol." The sisters wear a white sari with a blue border. The white represents purity. The three blue borders represent the Father, the Son, and the Holy Spirit. Blue is also the color of the Virgin Mary. The sisters' sari is a witness to mankind: it is the sign of God's love.